CELL MATE

CELL MATE

ANA MERINO

Translated by

ELIZABETH POLLI

Harbor Mountain Press
Brownsville, Vermont

Cell Mate originally appeared as *Companera de celda* (Visor Libros).
Harbor Mountain Press would like to express gratitude to Jesús García Sánchez
and Visor Libros for permission to publish this first English translation.
Please see www.visor-libros.com for more information
about Visor Libros titles, Madrid, Spain.

Harbor Mountain Press acknowledges the support of
Pentangle Council on the Arts (Woodstock, Vermont)
for this and other literary projects.

First printing 2007

ISBN 0-9786009-5-9

Series Editor:
Peter Money

Cover illustration:
Félix de la Concha

Production editing:
Barbara Jones

Harbor Mountain Press
Brownsville, Vermont
05037

www.harbormountainpress.com

Table of Contents

Captivity of Dreams

In memory of my grandfather Jerónimo

THE PRISONER'S DREAMS

The prison city has closed its doors
and you have remained inside
caressing the cold that chills the battlements.

This time you will dream about the truth that fills
a tiny blue vial
and the empty embrace of a lonely person.

You'll think that the essence of pain
lives inside you
like a fairy without wings
waiting for the future
to grant her a wish.

The prison city
at times takes control of your trembling lips
when you cry, fast asleep,
and no one cradles you in their arms.

They'll wake you up
the words you write
transformed into ants.
You'll see them undo every paragraph
and march around the walls of your cell
in thin, thin lines.

This time you'll dream that the city doesn't exist
and that poems are the only language
you have left.

Sometimes the words
build a nest in your throat
and they say what you think,
then you forget
that you are dragging the chains
of a lifeless city
where only your dreams
recognize the streets.

Sometimes we look at each other
you lean on my body,
a deformed gargoyle
and you sleep like an angel,
and I, who lie forever awake,
I envy you when you dream.

ROCK, PAPER, SCISSORS

Rock,
cold,
a silent corner
next to the lap of the dead.

Paper,
to write,
a few brief lines,
the rushed farewell
of the traveler.

Scissors,
to cut off the tongue of the sea
when it sighs.

Scissors,
to cut out the dreams
of the drowned.

Paper
to write down their names.

Rocky straights
little paper boat
scissor-like reefs.

A melancholy poem
for those who were left breathless
at the edge of the sea.

Stone tears
paper rafts
and the mouth of the sea
with scissor-like teeth.

A TINY ANGST

A secret corner
full of unfortunate truths.
Life abandons us as orphans
with a memory of a trail
one like the tail of a comet
or the footprints of a sleepwalker in the snow
who dreams that the cold
will make him invincible.

In the skin,
around the lips
tiny folds,
remnants of a time
of uncertain words;
a fist-full of promises
now a mere echo.
And love, like babble
leaves no trace at all.

DÉJÀ VU

Dream again
that your feet
fit into my shoes.

Don't be afraid of the time
you've spent
without brushing up against my shadow.

Your prison of words
doesn't matter,
my shoes
are full of you,
you are mine every time I walk
through your suicidal memory
of a lover condemned
to a perpetual broken heart.

Dream again
that I look at you
in the bathroom mirror,
and your embrace makes me
identical.

Don't be afraid of the time
you let pass by
each time my lips
evoked the secret trace
of you
hidden in a watch
shaped like a toy.

Dream again
that we crossed paths
in a desert full
of lizards and avocadoes,
and that early mornings turn into
our last dance.

Dream of me now
that you are old
and I dare seek you
without asking your permission
because you were my body
and your chains are my pain as well.

CITY OF SAND

To the girls of Ciudad Juárez

Oh that an imagined city
could wake up to be real.

That paradise could also
be built in the desert,
without the tree of life,
without demons, nor Adams
without God, only women
surrounded by angels.

Oh that paradise could be
a city of sand
where little girls could
grow up to be grandmothers.

CHILDREN'S WORK

At the crosswalks
a hand smiles
palm extended
the gaze is glassed over
from glue and dreams.

They wash our windows
with soapy water
and mouths smile
with crooked teeth
and swollen lips.

On the sidewalks
the dragons are children
their fire has a bitter taste,
they only fly at night
stuffing their heads
into paper bags.

With cans of paint
they imagine time
decorating the walls
of a jailed infancy.

In the heart of round-a-bouts
misfortunes pile up,
they mound up in plastic bags
and the children stare at us
with snake eyes.

Their prison is the street
their hangman the speed
of the cars that pass by.

THE FIFTH SKY

For Martín López-Vega

We will be children
when death brushes against the fifth sky.
We'll want to hug
the laughter that innocence leaves behind
on rooftops.

Cat meowing
that plans
to take over the space of shadows.
And we, we are debating
between trying to fly
and the twisted longing
of wanting to escape
from our own body.

We will be children
forgetting the odor that adults leave behind,
the trace of their fears
tied to misfortunes of others' lives.

Old age will be the echo
of the cliffs,
the murmur of the water tank
drinking up the silence of the night.

We will be good children
in white coffins
and we'll weave dreams
moistening the wicker
in thermal waters
of fairy tales.

NAKED ANGEL

I know that on some nights
you listen to my heart beat
dressed like the devil,
huddled in the shadows,
behind the manger in Bethlehem.

Your fingers caress me
because I am the figure
which brings in its hands
the bitterness of an angel
who wanted to be a god.

Naked, I am the statue
that keeps secrets
with tears of snow.
Naked, I am marble
and the murmur of the wind
makes itself at home in my mouth.

I know that on some nights
you listen to my heart beat,
dressed like the devil
and the angst forces you
to search inside my chest
for your own heart.

MONA LISA

You learn to look
with absent eyes
and your mouth condenses
quietude,
and the pleasure of knowing that you are painted
and that no one can imagine what you think.

You learn to exist
because they invent you on canvas,
and they fill the space between your lips
with light,
and they want to touch you
even though your face
is mere pigment.

You learn to be alive
because someone searches for you,
you hear their heart beat
as they admire you
and you breathe in the air their silence leaves behind.

You learn to be art,
that nothing hurts you,
that the universe be
your distant gaze
filling up with fog,
and your lips hold

the perfect smile,
the poisonous trace
of a woman who dreams
and who is broken inside.

DEATH BY SANITY

To Alonso Quijano the Goodheart

You have your wits again,
your being, the spell broken,
is exhausted
from knowing that it is mortal,
fragile and sane.

All that you believed
was only unfamiliarity
with familiar shadows
transformed into make-believe.

Books produced
the immortal breath
of those that live
spell-bound.

And you were invincible
imagining desire
in the empty words
of others' fears.

Now that sanity
is your epitaph
what you dreamed
can no longer exist,
I can no longer live
in your insanity,
dressed as a made-to-fit
mirror-image.

NIGHTIME WORSHIP

For Luis Muñoz

Let them give you Mondays back
and mark them holidays in your day book
so the week won't weigh as heavy on you
and so you can feel the teeth of the streets
nibble with tenderness
the last stretch of hours on Sunday.

Let them give you the hours of Mondays back
and you can safeguard them under the bed sheets
so the city will sleep in your lap
and so that those who look at you will get their fill.

Let them bring you the rhythm of dreams
and you'll dance to them,
and the light of your embrace
will keep a secret safe.

Let Mondays learn
your body by heart.

Let nothing be missing from your world
because the god of night
rested on Mondays
to wait for you.

DECIPHERING PARADISE

I'm deciphering paradise:
in case anyone asks,
it has grated coconut
mixed with sugar.

The gods fell asleep
cooking the present
and they became human,
waking up naked
in the old freezers
of a meat and fish market.

I'm deciphering paradise
adding a touch
of chicken broth.

When the freezers were cleaned out
the bodies
became mortal.

The ice melted into meat with fish scales
and the god of hope
tasted like swordfish to us.

I'm deciphering paradise
in case anyone eats
the eyes of rain
and wakes up crying like a child.

The meat fell apart
and the god that dreams about the world
woke up agonizing in a pot.

CHICKEN BROTH

In the airplanes
the engine is chicken broth;
the invisible logic
of the new pilots
finds an alternative fuel
that is cooked at home.

And wars
are merely the condiment
for things that are boiled
in ten minutes.

A sprig of bay leaf
from a crown
that didn't know how to reign.

And the palate of an ogre
who snores like a tiger
fills up with down feathers
spit out by the engines
of those new airplanes
that run
on a bit of broth.

Don't let the children
wake you up,
with your dreams we can change
the flavor of things.

We convert spoons
into airplanes with propellers
and sign peace agreements
with a baby's white bib.

ROOM ON THE NINTH FLOOR

Ninth floor
room of a naked woman
who has traded her wings
for the shade of summer
transformed into fine thread
embroidering blue scars
with her skin.

Silver lock
encrusted
in the carapace
of insects
that agonize
in their tiny cells
of outstretched legs and straight pins
caressing the sky.

Ninth floor
to fantasize from its cornice
the freedom of the archangels
spying on dreams
with vampire's teeth.

The breath of another life
captured in the embrace
of a white sheet
that wraps up
the agony of broken bones
on the gray earth
of the sidewalk.

Key to the transparent word
in the patio of laughter,
the abyss of childhood
that dissolves
in drops of mercury
and a fever falsified
in a yawn.

Ninth floor
of happiness
that never arrives,
noisy room of the echo
of television
dressed like a whimsical window.

Lock to the soft walls
with a needle for a key,
to live within oneself
amongst the frequency
of strange noises
and to wake up
transformed into a being
that has been a precipice.

TINY CONFESSION

If I am your dream
why do I feel alone
when you dream of me?

I arrive dragging my body
to your mouth when you sleep
and I don't know how to begin
to tell you a story
that looks like yours
so that you never know
that I live with you.

We dreams
are like shadows,
we belong to one single body
yet we yearn to be
somebody else.

Captivity of Shadows

To my girlfriends

SOMEONE WHO IS HAPPY

Someone who is happy
is like my wish
for small victories,
and has dreamed that he grows
with each mouthful
of desire fulfilled.

That sleeping giant
is the blue silhouette
of my defeat,
and now wanders
with a sleepwalker's clumsiness
outside
my lit-up house.

Someone who is happy
who wasn't invited
has impregnated with happiness
my small failure.
He has woken me up
in the midst of the snow
and made me cry out-loud that I am alive
for now.

THE MAN WHO TASTES LIKE CHOCOLATE

The man who tastes like chocolate
has fallen asleep.

His eyes,
made of bitter chocolate
blink, sometimes,
and the air gets thick
in his mouth of whipped cream,
in the liquid caramel of his lips.

My intuition tells me
that pure chocolate
cannot be a man,
that desire should not
draw such sweet mirages.

The man who tastes like chocolate
doesn't seem real,
I don't want him to be,
chocolate conceals
passions darker
than love.

PERFECT

In order to be perfect
I need to be boiled
with goat's milk.

I need the breath
of a naked shadow
that would want to stay next to my body,
that would remake my breasts,
that would kneed my waist
and would invent me with clay
if God would permit.

In order to be perfect
I should grow with the corn,
cling to the earth
so that the sun could draw my hips.

I'd have to wait
upon my gravestone
sewing in my entrails
the maps of desire.

I'd have to accept
the artisan hands
of a shadow with no owner.

In order to be perfect
I should die many times
without ceasing to live in the memory
of those who dream of me.

I'd have to be soul
boiling over low heat,
turned into caramel liquor.

TINY VANITY

Tiny vanity
that lives in my belly,
center of everything I say
when I concentrate
on my own smile.

I've seen with the skin
of giraffes
the world from above.

Tiny vanity
that is fed
by whimsical dreams,
and that wishes to be a nation
in the humble homeland
of my body.

Delirious, it asks me
for its own independence
embroidering with my blood
its flag.

Tiny vanity
who makes the mistake
of trying to get dressed
in my clothes.

Of wanting to write
its name in my epitaph
and erase from the earth
my tiny little mark.

FLAVOR CAPTURED

You cannot find it
even though you might smell its trace
in the ancient walls
of dreamed houses.

It's the flavor captured
that whispers it exists
in the sacred mouths
of blind angels.

It's a never-ending yawn
in which time keeps
silver baby's rattles
and tin soldiers.

It's a centipede with wings
that lives on the edge of anguish
and screws up its legs
wanting to escape
from its tiny jelly jar.

It's the saddest flavor
that the chef jots down
in a book of dishes and recipes,
that's why it's kept hostage
and it's only steamed with sorrow
and a few drops of blood
that the heart of Quetzalcoatl keeps within.

SPOONFULS

The pleasure
of chocolates and strawberries,
like a naked body
with bits of almonds
and a few droplets of honey.

Lips of truffles
and warm custard
with a little ice cream
and a rum-soaked cake.

The passion of burnt sugar
on top of whipped cream
of frozen desserts.

The panting
of wild blackberries
of egg whites beaten stiff
meringued in the oven.
A perverse spell
for the mouths
for insomniac palates
that even after making love
are still hungry.

HONEY MOON

For Marta and Alberto

Love shelters itself in suitcases
and learns to decipher
its own mechanism
so it won't make a mistake.

When it wants to travel
it melds itself into your hug
and it wants you to hope for
infinity.

It looks like you two
and sometimes it has dreamed
that it was in a box
with maps and thimbles
embroidering the universe
with a very fine thread.

Love buttons itself up
in the blue navel of desire
it fills you with caresses
it lives in each kiss
and it keeps in your breath
the true silence
of eternal things.

ALPHABET SOUP

b-e-a-c-h
An embrace of the sea is suicide
that sometimes the rocks
on the beach savor.

c-r-y-s-t-a-l
A kiss of crystal
is almost always sad
because it has the tendency to break into pieces.

c-r-i-c-k-e-t-s
The echo of the night
is the essence of crickets
under a pillow.

c-o-o-k p-o-t-s
Maple sap
drips in the cook pot
and the heat purifies its bitterness.

c-a-t-a-r-a-c-t-s
In the eyes
a cloud of tiny sky
disguises itself as shade.

k-a-p-o-r-i-s
Fills the pillows
with down feathers
to sleep without guilt.

h-a-t-r-e-d
Enemies dream
that hatred is factory made
and sells at a high price.

d-i-s-h
Some read the future
in a soup dish
that holds false letters.

KOSHER FASCINATION

I look for you in the kitchen
and I find you organizing
two refrigerators,
one for milk
and the other for meat,
each flavor dressed
in its own set of dishes.

You never eat eggs
that have tears of blood
in the yolks.

In the sea that is your mouth
the only thing that fits are fish with scales,
fish that don't have fins.

To know is to fear infinity,
to diminish the trace
that wounds leave,
and to savor the good fortune
of a table set
where love is never wanting.

SOLOMONIC METHOD

Divide truth
in two halves,
add zest of lemon
to the driest part,
look for the darkest side
to sweeten it up.

Let them cook,
mix them with corn meal
and thoughts of lava from the volcano,
stir slowly
so lumps won't form
and so the bottom doesn't burn.

Wait for however long
it takes,
until the words
turn back into appetite
and hunger transforms us
into silent silhouettes.

Chew each piece
convinced
of the truth
on the table,
served piping hot
on a plate of shadows

decorated with tiny flowers
and dead grasshoppers.

And eat it all,
even if we only believe half of it.

AUTUMN RECIPIES

Infusion of licorice,
cat's claw,
caress autumn,
let the wind of dry leaves
curl up
inside your belly.

Caress the navel
of the trees
turned into moss
of trunks cut off.

Infusion of anisette
rose water,
bundle up the kids
who have no memory,
let them curl up
inside your belly of spikes.

To be reborn after a snowfall,
to be reborn with the subtle cold of death
shivering in your mouth.

Let them rub your arms and legs,
let them embrace you
and ask you to stay.

Infusion of sea water
to forget that narrow streets
and kisses that tasted like doorways
existed.

Caress the yawn
of children who dream,
give them watches
so they can play at living in time.

Infusion of old clothes,
cake of scars
and drops of patience
that smell like fear.

BASEMENT 7B

The axis of dreams
is half-buried in my office.
Next to the file cabinet that hides my disorder
of old documents, day planners I haven't used,
dried up pens
and strips of paper that on one day I wrote
the key to a language that never found its voice
and will die with me.

Underneath three small glass vials
that stored the salts of life
the metal of an obsolete machine
sticks out,
that was the axis of time
when no one knew how to measure it with clocks,
then, a thousand stories were told
which invoked the stars
and dreams tasted like
vanilla cream pudding
or lemon sorbet in the summer.

Underneath a carpet
covered with mites and stains
they traced the signs
which measure the distance
between love dreamed
and love lived,

as if passion were an invention
that sleepwalkers dream
and learn to imitate trapeze artists
when the net that prevents suicide
isn't there.

Underneath my feet
the universe was dreamed
when the alchemists
wanted to distil infinity
and achieve that its essence
made us immortal.

Underneath my shadow,
in the desolate hole with no light that is my office
the impossible happened.
Now that I know,
I won't ask to change.

CELL MATE

Don't force me to live
as if every instant
were the work piled up,
that we leave until the last minute.

If you want to be my body
don't steal my peace of mind
nor the shadows of the afternoon
which appear through the mist
of an enchanted forest.

I have run away, so many times, from you,
but you are always at my side.
Your knees, and the way I cry,
your hands, and my sweat,
your eyes and my gaze.

Don't force me to live
thinking that you don't feel like
growing old with me,
that I exist in you because of your inertia
that it doesn't matter to you that it hurts me
to know you are so fragile.

I've tried to ignore you,
to avoid the sensation
in your fingers
when they feel the foreignness
of gray matter.

My distress,
like a ghostly breath
clings to the dream of life
and learns to smile
with your mouth at the doctors.

If you want to be my body
let me fall asleep under your eyelids,
dream that we are one,
and that you won't betray me
on the operating table,
that you are going to wake up with me
from the same nightmare,
and you're going to feel that I am
more alive than ever, in your throat.

Don't force me to grow up
learning to read
the map of scars on your body,
I don't want to recognize one more wound
nor do I want you to confuse
a broken heart with the illnesses
and the knots of fever.

Don't let your body pay for my sins
in the blue drowning of the oceans,
let the distance be
a metal clock and an afternoon of snow
where life would want
to learn to kiss me with your lips.

FINAL PRISON

Prisoner
life rocks you
like a child
who cries in distress
who drools with the pain
of cutting teeth.

It looks like it has snowed
a drunken foam
on the reddish gums
of your mouth.

Your language
is just the babble
of a shadow grown old
in the vast prison
of the streets.

Prisoner
night time takes you hostage
with its breath
of wet ice
touching your face,
and dreams rock you
like a new-born baby
who feels infinity
in the indescribable abyss
of his cry.

TINY SCAR

I write because I have
the scar of dreams
inside my head.

A dry blow
of words,
drips of scattered ideas
and the loss of memory dressed
as a girl who sleepwalks
who stumbles with the future
and who falls in the present
damp with piss and old sweat.

I write because sometimes
my scar doesn't dream,
and its insomnia
frightens me.

Ana Merino was born in Madrid, Spain in 1971. She is an
Assistant Professor at Dartmouth College, where she teaches Spanish
and Latin American Literature and Culture. She has published five
books of poetry, *Preparativos para un viaje* (1995), *Los días gemelos*
(1997), *La voz de los relojes* (2000), *Juegos de niños* (2003) and *Compañera
de celda* (2006); a scholarly book on comics titled *El Cómic Hispánico*
(2003) and a critical monograph on Chris Ware (2005). The recipient
of the Adonais and Fray Luis de León awards for poetry, she was also
awarded the Diario de Avisos Award for best critical short articles
about comics for the Spanish literary magazine, *Leer*. Merino is a
member of the executive committee for the International Comics Art
Forum (ICAF) and a member of the board of directors for the
Center for Cartoon Studies in White River Junction, Vermont. She
has served as curator for three comics exhibitions, one in the United
States and two in Spain.

Elizabeth (Chamberlain) Polli was born in Springfield,
Massachusetts in 1958. After completing her B.A. at the University
of Colorado, Boulder, she moved to Madrid, Spain, where she taught
English for six years at what was then the most prestigious American
language school in Spain, La Asociación Cultural Hispano-
Norteamericana. She began translating in Madrid when she was
hired to work at a small art-film distribution house, producing
subtitles in both English and Spanish for a variety of foreign language
films released in Spain. In 1997 she earned her Ph.D. from Columbia
University and is currently the Spanish Language Program Director
in the Department of Spanish and Portuguese at Dartmouth
College, Hanover, New Hampshire.